(un) DOCUMENTED

My Story, My Journey, MY TRUTH

(un) DOCUMENTED

My Story, My Journey, MY TRUTH

DelShanna Moore

(un) DOCUMENTED: My Story, My Journey, MY TRUTH

Unless otherwise noted, all Scripture quotations are taken from the King James Version of the Bible © 1988 by Liberty University.

The italicized emphasis in Scripture quotations is added by the author.

Cover Design: Ginisis Media Group
Editor: Christy Cumberlander-Walker
Co-Editors: Dr. Kathy Howard and Derrick Moore

Table of Contents

Dedication

This book is dedicated to every boy and girl, man and woman who has been mishandled, misunderstood, and mistreated. May you embrace your experiences and stand in your truth.

Love yourself as your story writes your future. Find peace and joy along your journey. Tell your truth, the way you tell it. Be you, undeniably, inexcusably perfect.

I will tell the world who I am Unapologetically Authentically ME!

Acknowledgements

My husband for his undying support and understanding.

My parents for their unconditional love.

My pastors for their acceptance and truth.

My family for their shoulders to lean on.

My sisters and brothers in Christ for their listening ears and prayers.

My mentors for their advice and strength.

My children for their unspoken unconditional love.

Special Thanks

To all those who supported this project by pre-ordering, I thank you from my heart.

Robertha Towels	Kechia English
Olivia Brown	Craig McNair
Sara' Thomas	Donnel Moore
Veronica Matlock	Sharon Watson
Diana White	Dwayne Roberts
Ebony Hall	Teesha Dorsette
Connie Jones	Gregory S. Young
Sandra Martinez	Carolyn Rogers
Frances 'Tish' Bowman	Sabrina Davis
Gabriyelle Gaines	Tyra Welch
Sherry Traylor	Stefanie Toney
Hubzetta Pernell	Cynthia Thomas
MicShaun Jones	Latasha Jimerson
Royal Cooper	Thelma Douglas
Melissa Armstrong	Marlon Neal
Malysa Heffner	Best Decision
Phaedra Barrett	Gracie Harris
Stella Landry	Maya Cotton
Wonswayla Mackey	Altoria May
Phyllis Collier	Robin Franklin
Devonta Haney	Jameela Morris
Brandy Hunt	Angela Mackey
Anjanette McBath	Gayus Conley
Racheal Frazier	Tiffany Yancy
MarQuee Munday	Eugenia "Genia" Woods-Rosa

Introduction

It was not long before I knew something was wrong with me. It took even less time to discover something was wrong with all of us. People of all cultures were having similar experiences and telling similar stories. It was their story. It was their journey. It was their truth.

There is a story to tell about the journey that is set for you and the journey we choose to travel in life. The story is not always fun and most definitely includes suffering and disappointment, oftentimes abuse and degradation. Along the journey we discover ourselves. As we travel the roads and corridors of early living, we uncover ourselves. In the process, we find a truth. The truth that others tell and believe about us. The truth that we believe about others and most importantly and most devastatingly, our truth about ourselves.

This story is about a woman who lives undocumented. No one ever told her story. No one ever knew her story. Even though her story was their story and her life were theirs.

Undocumented is a phenomenon of people who live their lives in the margins of the narrative. They suffer the dangers of death and experience the realities of life, trauma, pain, and love. They shy away from truth and hide under the shadows of someone else's story, someone else's truth, and allow their journey to remain undocumented.

Awakened from my own trauma, I decided to stop hiding from who I was and remove the covers. I stopped running from my past and future and took the time to grab them both by the neck, look them straight in the face and declare that my story will be told in my life, my journey will be fulfilled and my truth shall be mine to tell.

Let these words provoke the opportunity to live aloud in your truth, uncovered, unhidden, undocumented.

Undocumented

In most countries, documents reflect your citizenship. They are the papers that communicate your rights and privileges. They disclose your "belonging" status. These papers give you permission to move on or return from whence you came. Whether it is a passport, certificate of birth or existence, license or identification card, most laws, local and abroad, always require you to carry documentation of some sort on your person. In fact, in my home state, if you are found absent required documents on your person it is a crime.

When you encounter law enforcement or government officials, they will always ask to see your documents. It is what is used as verifiable legitimate proof that you are who you say you are. Without a legal government issued document, you are labeled illegal, alien and/or undocumented.

When you are undocumented, your history, connections and status are unknown. Should we trust you? Are you a danger to others? Who are you, really? The uncertainty of who you are heightens security and creates an offensive situation that must be resolved almost immediately. Action required, NOW!

To be undocumented causes you to be arrested, deported, and misunderstood. Let's dig into this.

Undocumented causes your arrest. Arrested development is a common perspective of hindered growth. It is to have your development: your growth, your access, your lessons, your knowledge, your worth: held up, impeded upon, stopped, detained, shut down, locked up, and blocked. While some consider your incarceration necessary to ensure proper transport and residence, it is used for your safety during times of uncertainty.

While most can relate to people being arrested for crimes, we must understand arrests result in detention. These include the detaining of your development. You cannot grow while confined and surrounded by bars. Your life will be controlled, your goals narrow, and your destiny becomes restricted.

Undocumented causes your deportation. Abrupt removals from your home causes a traumatic imprint in your heart and mind.

Trauma is birthed and breeds fear in where you are and where you go next. Being moved from a place of comfort and familiarity to being placed in an unknown place without preparation thwarts progression.

While being detained awaiting deportation, documents could prove your existence, documents could prove your necessity, documents prove you have the right to be here.

The documents identify you have access. Without them, even though others see you, they will discredit your importance and silence your voice. They will treat you beneath human decency and neglect your ability to represent yourself.

A stranger will be given rights over your life and dictate where you go, what you eat and what you will do. Goals, what goals? The strange overseer now determines your goals and with the help a few rules (laws) and standards (culture), your goals ae smashed to the bottom of their boots, and tread upon like disrespected dirt.

Undocumented causes you to be misunderstood. Without proper documentation people do not know who you really are. They will misunderstand your role, responsibilities, purpose, and participation. Why? Because they can only ascertain your gifts, purpose, and existence from their framework, through the examination of documents.

It is easy to consider someone's talents by what you have seen them do, but when they are promoted two and three levels, suspicion sets in because their documents were not visible or on display. They are misunderstood because no one knew they were qualified for more. Without visible, publicized documents, who we are is disguised, hidden and unclear.

Documents are necessary. Like the word of God that leaves an inheritance from generation to generation, the printing and written information left behind on tablets and in other forms provide the evidence that you are who you say you are.

What documents do you have that identify your God given birth right? What do your documents prove about you? Take a moment and review the documents you have on yourself, your spouse and loved ones. What message do they give?

My brokenness and loneliness were undocumented. So was my fear and anxiety. When I would snap at people or crawl in my safety blanket, they did not understand why I was running away or why I became invisible in the crowd. When I would take offense or 'clap' back, it was difficult for others to understand why I was so angry or why I was not as friendly as our initial encounter.

When I would turn away and separate myself altogether, they were unaware I was hurting and bleeding and trying to get help for those awful memories of heart break and childhood abuse. They did not see my documents, the documents of my testimony, trials, and troubles.

They did not know I was broken because they had only seen the documents that expressed my existence through joy, peace, and happiness. A smile is what they always saw. Positive and encouraging responses is what they always record. So, to experience something different was strange, bizarre, and unembraceable.

I did not show them all my documents. I did not tell them about my other documents. I made sure they had access to the necessary documents, it did not matter. Those preliminary documents did not prevent them from prejudging me harshly or rejecting me. When I proved who I was, the treatment did not change. All additional documents brought to the table to prove my worth were ignored. Unfortunately, because they did not know who I was I remained misunderstood, like most that are undocumented.

I remained arrested in those circles. They excluded me from the conversation, ignored my suggestions and demeaned my contribution to the process. It became clear that they were stuck in their image of who should have the solution. They expected the most favorable words to be released out of the mouth of someone that looked or sounded like me. Because of their prejudices, they ignored and missed the person near them who was answering their questions and had the resolution.

Like Jesus Christ, they were there, right next to me, experiencing my capabilities hearing my knowledge and examining the precision of gifts. But they too, kept me undocumented.

Despite their push, there was an awareness when I traveled through the system of my life.

Those afar and above, saw me, knew me, and heard me. My credentials were already reviewed, and my secrets were not hidden from them. When I was not watching, and when I thought no one knew my name, they had written my name down in their notes to reference later.

Experience after experience, I became documented. A little piece here, a little more there. From the superficial façade and pain suffering smile to the talents buried behind my protective shield and shame. They saw me, they knew me, they heard me.

It was "them" that refused to acknowledge my documents. It was the other "them" who happily received my documents. And just like that, my story was written, my journey was revealed, and my truth was told. Not as their story, not intertwined with their truth and not inclusive of their journey. It was my story, my journey, and my truth, finally, documented.

My

Story

Invisible

It is a common question when looking for someone. "Where is she?" "Where did she go?" "I thought she was here, but I don't see her."

When scanning a crowd or looking out from the midst of a crowd, many times you wonder where is the person that was with you. It is not because they are not there, but because they are out of your sight. They may or may not be in your purview, but oftentimes, she is still there, in the room, in the vicinity, nearby or like me, right next to you.

I recall attending meetings and programs accompanied with a group. The leaders were conversing with leaders and workers with workers. I would stand nearby, but afar in my spirit and mind. As the time would progress, soon someone would come looking for me, "Where is she?" I would stand even closer as they continued to look about wondering where I was. Considering if I had left. The truth is I was standing near them, in plain view and even at times right next to them.
"Invisible," they called me. Invisible.

I had this unplanned ability to disappear in a room. I heard the conversation. I acknowledged the comical review and search for agreement. But while my presence was physically evident, I was unnoticed otherwise. They did not feel me. They did not hear me. I was breathing. I was there. But they could not see me.

The act of invisibility was popular in childhood cartoons and cool animated movies or science fiction films. Having some sense of supernatural power encourages a man with a special potion or emotion that would allow them to intentionally turn on their disappearing power and become invisible to the naked eye. It was magic! It was superpowers! It was supernatural! It was a cartoon, imagination and not real.

Until they met me.

One evening after a meeting, I entered the room with executive leadership. They shared intimate details about their mutual comrades and partners. I stood until I tired and then sat nearby, as usual. An hour and a half passed when one leader saw me and requested my removal to prevent me from having access to the intimate information being shared. She did not know I was there the entire conversation and I heard everything they talked about. She was uncomfortable and I left the room.

What was that? It was a superpower I learned from childhood. It is a great, yet awful reminder of how I internalized my abuse. How I believed that my presence wasn't important, and my connection wasn't required. No one cares about me, or what I had experienced. I told myself this as a child and then allowed this self-fulfilling prophesy to become my mantra as an adult. I looked for opportunities to disappear and every time, all those people who'd said they loved me and wanted me, would lose me in the room, not even see me in the room, not even feel me sitting or standing right next to them. I was quiet. I stayed quiet.

I thought it was cute for a while. How I could be alone amid company. How I could leave the room while at a banquet table with talkative guests. I did it often. I did it always. I did not expect anyone to invite me in. I did not expect anyone to include me. I had spent so much time at the table without anyone interested in my opinion or what I had to say that I simply became comfortable being discounted and ignored. I expected to be dismissed and insignificant. So instead of reaching out to them, I disappeared, at the table, in the room, next to them.

One day a woman called me by name and invited me to the table. She did not like that I was sitting alone. She found something odd and unacceptable about that. However, once I joined the table, I disappeared. They never saw me again!

I never left the room. I never left the table. But what I realized is that it was too hard to connect to people. It took too much work to join their team. So, I disappeared to prevent being disappointed in them. I disappeared to prevent being misunderstood. I disappeared to prevent being hurt, again.

The appreciation of this defense mechanism was a gift at times. When working with public officials it was imperative to be invisible. I had to work a room and do so without making a scene, deflecting attention, or interrupting a program or event. I had to move from the back of the room to the front of the stage without drawing any attention and I did it so effortlessly it became a wanted skill for others working in my capacity.

How to teach it? It took years of negative self-talk, proven self-prophesies and an internal dysfunction that would cause more damage than it was worth. People did not understand what they were missing. They had no idea what they were getting, and they would never know what it cost to deliver the invisible girl, alone in the crowd, unheard, unseen, unknown... undocumented.

*When doubt shows up, smother it
with the endless possibilities of your faith.
Oh yes, you can!*

Don't Touch Me

If I had a choice. If I had a voice.
Instead I can only imagine my rebuttal and
disagreement. What does Don't touch me
sound like?

Umm, what are you doing?

Hey wait a minute... no, wait... umm

Don't touch me.

No.

Stop.

I said no.

Hey, no. No. NO!!!

... I said stop it.

No!

Helpless

Ugh… ugh… ugh…

Weeping…

Scrubbing my body

Crying

I said No, don't touch me, stop.
…
…
…
…
…

Unheard.

Nobody Heard My Cry

I was 5 and I cried, but no one heard me.

I was 7 and I cried, but no one heard me.

I was 9 and I cried, but no one was listening.

I was 11 and I cried and was told to "shut up, you are making too much noise."

I was crying. I cried at night. I cried during the day. I cried every time I knew he was going to be here. I cried every time he left. I cried. I cried alone.

The visible tears of a child were mistaken for being a spoiled brat or a 'cry baby'. Those were the loud cries, the public cries. But the silent tears were only evident by the tear stained pillowcases and salted residue upon my cheek in the morning. Who cared? Who was listening?

I cried.

I cried like so many hurting people cry today.

I cried for attention, in hopes that someone would look my way, acknowledge my pain, and realize I was shouting, "I AM HERE!"

I cried for help. Awaiting my savior, the ones sent to protect me and rescue me to see that if their eyes would connect with mine for just a moment I could ask, or I would say, "I need your help. Help me!"

I cried for love. Hoping that one day, he would see me beyond what my physical body could satisfy. He would appreciate me and validate me as a person not an object. If only he would look at me, instead of through me I could ask him…

"Am I enough for your love? Do you love me?"

I cried for shelter. A place where I could be safe, free from harm and the harsh realities of life on the outside. A dwelling place to be my haven, my home with built-in comforts and protective shields from harm and enemies.

"Will anyone give me a safe place to stay."

I cried for anyone. "Does anyone hear me? Is anyone there?"

*I have an ear for their cry. I can hear the cry
and I have the power to help.*

Not Like That

To have his attention was cool. He was cute. The other girls had a cute guy, I wanted one too. He was a couple of years older than I, but it was okay. He was cute, you know.

The other kids played a different game. They ran and hid and touched each other. They touched me. I liked him and I wanted him, but not like that.

Then there was the other guy, who was to be off limits, right? I thought so. I thought everyone thought so. He played that game, too. Somehow, I was the slow one. I was always stuck, him and me, alone, in the dark room, no way out. He touched me and I did not like it. I did not want it, not like that.

Later he was in my house and then in my bedroom touching me. I never asked him to touch me. I never signed up for the game, but there he was again, touching me… that way I did not like to be touched… not like that.

I Can't Feel

There are times I cannot feel the pain of others because pain is everywhere. There are times when I guard my heart from the realities of others' stories because it is just too hard to feel. It is difficult accepting how an adult man will penetrate the innocence of a toddler. It is unbearable to realize how a mother will sell her child for drugs. It is unfathomable to realize how a father will beat his child to death. It is too hard to realize how a mother will kill her child and stuff her in a duffle bag, trash can or 3-foot grave. It is just too hard to realize how true the story is.

It is too hard to understand and I do not want to believe that a human being with a spirit and a soul could do such things without remorse, without some sense of guilt or shame, without the need to apologize. Yet, every day, I experience another story of parents failing at protecting their gift and how other adults failed to protect their dynasty to a moment of personal lustful desire, costly desires only the innocent virtue of a child would satisfy.

Do not say, "I'll pay you back for this wrong!"
Wait for the LORD, and he will avenge you.
Proverbs 20:22

Secret Makers

There is something about having a secret that makes you nervous. You want to tell it, but there is a tightening in your belly that prevents you from saying a word. Maybe it is because you were threatened or thought you would get in trouble. Maybe it is because you were simply told to be quiet and as a child you did as you were told; or maybe it was because you trust and honor the secret maker.

Oh, the lies they tell. The horror they inflict. The futures they distort for that story, that exposition called a secret.

What should we do with the secret maker? Should they be destroyed or blown away? Should they be mishandled in desperate revenge? Should they experience public humiliation for acts committed long ago? What should be done to the secret maker?

Making secrets that tear the innocence of little children and burn the backsides of tomorrows dreamers. They create secrets to scold the just and mute the rambunctious vocal cords   of   musically   divine   moments.

What should we do with the secret, the secret
maker, and his babies?

Those who have survived childhood or
adulthood victimization walk through the
process of retribution and revenge. Even those
who were beaten to silence or scared to death,
they awaken and desire justice for past
wrongdoings. The law can sometimes support
such efforts to bring people to justice.

However, I have seen over 40 years of
fighting back has brought the American culture
to continue to blame the victim, find reasons to
side with the perpetrator and dismantle the hope
for justice.

We have a choice! We could choose to stick
with the status quo, or we could do something
different. What will you choose to do with the
secret makers?

Connection

I saw something that I did not like.

I heard something that was not right.

I felt something that was uncomfortable.

I know something they do not know.

I

See

You.

*Do not give them more grace
than God would
nor love them less
than God does.*

Listen

Listen! Listen to me!

Did you hear me say that?
It was the failure of you hearing me. That was
why you did not know what was going on. Your
ears were out of tune. Your ears did not hear my
pain, my cry, my screams. Did you know me at
all?

Listen. If you just give me a chance to
respond, a chance to explain, we can talk
through it and both understand better. But you
would rather be right. You would rather take this
moment to degrade and discount my efforts, my
intentions, my willingness to try to make this
work. It does not matter if it is a relationship, a
job, or a conversation with a stranger. What have
you to gain by not listening to me? Are you
going to wait for me to answer the question?

Well, I learned from the best, how not to
listen. I learned to keep talking and talking and
talking. Were we arguing? I do not know, but if
I kept talking until all my thoughts were out and

all my language was exhausted, maybe this time, this stage, this open moment, you will hear me.

There is a sound in relationships that require quietness. Without that quietness, you'll never hear me, and you may not even see me. I cannot ask for what I need. I do not have the language, the courage to tell you, "Hey Bozo, shut up and listen!" Instead, I smile and let you ask questions and talk yourself into answers that never came from my mouth or my thoughts.

You are so devoid of empathy and justice that you would continue in your privileged conversation acting like you want my perspective, but really you do not. Hmmm, I need to be heard.

I need you to hear me by action or voice, you choose. If you do not hear my voice, you will hear my actions. I will move! I will go away. I will stay away. I will ignore you. I will respond, but not in the way you anticipate.

It hurts when I can enter a room and join a conversation, but still not be heard. Why am I here? Why did you summons me to this meeting if you were going to shut down my ideas, silence my contributions or steal my inalienable right to speak?

I cannot call it. But I need to break out! My talk shifts negatively and I begin to complain and reference every experience from a negative perspective. What was happening? This is not me.

It is a trigger. It was my trigger!

Because I felt unheard as a child and incapable of speaking up, when it is done to me in adulthood, I turn into that little girl almost instantly. She responds immaturely to the situations and the receptors look confused and bewildered. What is going on?

I am hurt. I am hurt and the wound of my childhood abuse is opened and bleeding again. Even though I do not know them well and our relationship is superficial, professional at best. Why the pain? Why am I back here? Why is that little girl back here?

Because they refuse to LISTEN!

Come to me, all you who are weary and burdened, and I will give you rest. Take my yoke upon you and learn from me, for I am gentle and humble in heart, and you will find rest for your souls. For my yoke is easy and my burden is light. Matthew 11:28-30 (NIV)

It's Not Over

I went through a series of healing processes as a college student. I came face to face with the demons of being molested and made a conscious decision that I was not going to let them hold me back. I went to therapy. I read books. I did research. I practiced good touch and saying no. I ran away from my family. I hid in another state. I was not going to suffer from the memories of all the pain anymore.

What was most helpful for me was the research. I found out that children molested have the same cry. While they cannot all articulate the violation, they demonstrate the fear and warning of danger. One pamphlet I read reflected the warning signs of a child in trouble. It suggested whining, fear, crying, even when the perpetrator was near. It included how children would come up with sicknesses to stay close to a safe adult, such as having an illness or physical complaint to prevent the safe caregiver from leaving them alone with the perpetrator. I agreed as I read those words in that pamphlet. I was angry when I read those words in that pamphlet.

Of the several warning signs, I exhibited all of them when the babysitter would come over. Why did no one hear my cry? I closed that pamphlet on recognizing the signs of sexual abuse, shut down my heart and moved on.

Therapy was helpful because it allowed me to talk about the molestation, at least to start talking about the abuse, details, emotions, fears. I talked about how I was hurt. I talked about how others tried to tell but they were ignored. Because no one believed them, I did not even have the guts to tell. The greatest advise through that process was to read about healing. I wrote a lot back then. Journals and notebooks held my deepest thoughts, secrets, desires, and hate. I wrote detailed descriptions of incident after incident, rape after rape, game after game, in detail. I even wrote my perpetrator a letter.

One day in therapy, I ripped it up. It was symbolic. It was tough. I cried just thinking about ripping it up. I cried as I ripped it up. I cried after I ripped it up. Why? I am not sure. Maybe because symbolically I was cutting off a familiar barrier in my life and giving myself permission to live. Or maybe it was because I did not know how to replace my pain with fresh air. Or maybe it was because what hurt me was also what protected me!

I cried and then I went on to live my life. It was true. I did not know what to put there. So, I had this hole in my life and just stuffed it with food, irresponsibility, social groups, and new friends from all over the world. I was having fun. I thought I was having fun. Then a memory returned, and I felt fear that my child would be hurt. I felt the violation all over again. Back to therapy I went.

This time I discovered it was not over. I found myself having strange experiences and running back to research and therapy. I felt empty. I was afraid. I was alone. I was afraid to be alone. I worked through going to a restaurant alone. I worked through enjoying a movie alone. I worked through protecting my son. I worked through trusting people.

I accepted that I could trust my instincts. I knew who to trust and those who were distrustful. That inside voice had proven its trustworthiness before and I could trust my voice. I could trust my intuition, my inner sound and feelings that reveled in the presence of another. I worked through fighting back. I worked through the blame... it was not my fault! It was not my fault! IT WAS NOT MY FAULT!!!

I learned the difference between good touch and bad touch. Bad touch was how he touched me, unwanted, unwarranted, unsatisfied, dirty, and unforgettable. Good touch was the touch I desired, a touch that I willfully engaged and encouraged. It was satisfying, pleasing, and embraced.

As an adult, ready to heal and be whole, I wanted to be touched in a good way. I wanted to feel good by the touch the touch of him, the touch of her, and the touch of me. I practiced good touch and I found enjoyment in welcoming good touch. It changed the type of people that I connected with. It changed the type of relationships I entered. It changed me!

But as I matured, I began to experience the wounds of my childhood. As far as I thought I had come, I felt like I was at the beginning again. I read enough books, went to enough therapy, talked enough through it and wrote enough about it, but I never cried about the grief that comes with having my virtue stolen or the grief of a lost childhood or the grief that stole my heart and my innocence. I cried this time like someone had died. I cried for a whole day. Every moment a new thought would cause tears to swell up in my eyes. Every thought would connect to another and the tears would roll down my cheeks. Yes, I cried.

My ultimate lesson was that there are levels to healing from childhood abuse, sexual abuse especially. There is not a pill to take or a recipe to fix it overnight. Probably because what happened to me, did not happen over a night. It was years of trouble that manifested in touch, fondling, and intercourse, fear, distrust, and self-protection. How silly to think it would all go away in a day, after a therapy session or after the reference list of a self-help book.

I decided to forgive! Yes, in all the work I had done true forgiveness has never manifested until I walked with God in the cool of the day. I practiced forgiveness in my present life, but I had not forgiven all those involved with the abuse from my childhood. Just as a peacock walks through the encasement, with quiet strength, I walked through my list of willing and involuntary participants that played a role in my distorted sense of self, the erosion of my innocence and the destruction of my safety.

I do not know if my healing process will ever be over. Even now I have exposure to children being hurt and a rage comes up inside of me to castrate the perpetrators. When I hear of victims of sex trafficking and pedophilia, I search myself for ways to eradicate every level of participation in the sex slave industry.

I thank God I got free! I was not a slave! It could have been me, though! So maybe my getting over my abuse is to fight against sex crimes on children, vulnerable teens and confused young adults.

I do not know if my healing journey will ever end, but I know I am consciously on it, keeping in the purview of a better way and a better tomorrow... one day at a time.

My

Journey

Chameleon Shift

I do not know when it happened. Suddenly, I could transform into this person who had the personality fitted for the moment. It was another one of those superhero powers from the cartoons, or the latest unstoppable and indispensable superhero who saved the world, again and again and again. Like a character in a scripted film, I learned how to be who they wanted me to be.

It was easy. When I entered the room, I would be jovial. By some attraction, I would join in conversation with people who were intelligent and there I was, speaking as one intelligent. In other instances, I would join a crowd who were hip but frank and there I was, accepting and like-minded.

In meetings, I would cover up my true opinion and align with the opinions of others. And just like that, I resembled their appearance. I looked like them. I resembled their voice intonations. I sounded like them. The comradery was true. I did care. I did believe in them and in their mission, but it was always disappointing that they failed to see me. They could not hear me.

No one missed the real me. That authentic Pollyanna type free loving spirit. In fact, I am not even sure they knew me (deviant smile). I mean, that was the point, was not it? To be hidden amid the crowd and look like I belonged until it was safe to show my true colors, my real personality, and talk in my own language. It was easy, until it was not.

I came in contact with a group of authentic people who did not want me to be them or be like them but expected to hear my untainted perspective and believed in me, as I had believed in so many others. They wanted me, her, DelShanna, the true DelShanna.

I am not sure I really knew how to be me. It took some time. There were trials and errors. I had to test them out and determine if they were trustworthy and faithful enough to be trusted with who I was and who I am.

Could I trust them with me?

So many had bargained my essence with their perversion, greed, lust, and ambitions. Was I worth real love, friendship, and partnership? What would it take this time to have a real friend, a true partner or real love? The type of love that does not go away when I have a tantrum or a flashback from my childhood. The type of love that embraces my social persona as well as my private secret sad self. The type of relationship that allowed them to be them and me to be me, Could I have that? Could we coexist on the same space and still be friends? A friendship where people would ask, "Where is DelShanna because the one who is talking is not her."

When people saw me, I mean really saw me, they knew who I was. They connected with my authenticity and electricity and embraced me. These people, these friends and partners did not always know how to love me or attend to me, but they always knew when I was absent, missing in the crowd or covering up to be someone else. It was that gift again. The one that was built on the inside of the abused child that restores a sense of self-worth and strength, self-preservation, and self-protection. The gift to be invisible and disappear in plain sight. No not that gift, this was the gift to camouflage myself amid the crowd and be what was safe to be in the room. The gift of the chameleon was a gift that kept me asking myself, "Where is she?"

The Chameleon Shift.

There is nothing I can do to make Christ love me more. I am not my shame and guilt. I am worth love, life, and death to Christ.
I am enough!

Babies Speak

If the babies could speak, what would they say?
If the babies could speak.

If the babies could speak, what would they
describe? If the babies could speak.

If the babies could speak, what would they
explain? If the babies could speak.

If the babies could speak, what would they tell?
If the babies could speak.

If the babies could speak, what would they
publicize? If the babies could speak.

If the babies could speak, what would they
disclose? If the babies could speak.

If the babies could speak, what would they
confess? If the babies could speak.

If the babies speak, secrets would be revealed.
If the babies could speak.

If the babies could speak, maybe they would say nothing at all, grin and walk away. If only the babies could speak.

I Was Born for More

It was a sermon. A powerful exhortation of God's promise to me. I sat in church that Sunday and received every word that was spoken as if I were the only person in the 2000 seat auditorium. I agreed. I concurred. Surely, I was born for more than where I was and what I had. There was greater in store for me.

There was a match that lit a fire on my inside. The type of fire that startled my old self because a new self was forming! I was not comfortable with what was happening in my life. I was not satisfied with the circumstances of my marital status: kind of single, kind of not. I was not happy with my life. So, I started standing up. I stood up to my house and threw out old stuff and began to organize and shed from years pass. What was important to me in my past no longer fit neatly in my dwelling space. It had to go!

I began finding my voice at work and realizing I could confess what I did well and ask for help to gain access to more knowledge and skill in my field. Things were changing. I was changing.

I was selected to attend a special program that solidified this transition in my life. I experienced emotional healing from being molested and came face-to-face with men and women who arrived as gap fillers, intercessors for the hurtful trauma of my past. Yes, pure strangers apologized for the attacks on my body, the lack of safety and trust from childhood trauma, the identity crisis I faced every day of my life as a girl, as a woman. Yes, they stood before me, as willing vessels and said, "DelShanna, I'm sorry."

I had never heard that before. I had never felt that before. I had never... they listened to me. They heard me. They acknowledged my pain as real and my trauma as horrific and undeserving. It was not my fault. I could build, grow, and expand in this space with pure strangers.

With overwhelmed emotions I called an old friend, a friend with benefits, that is. And I had someone who I could talk to, who would listen to me and hear me out and help me process all that I was dealing with. The night ended and the usual offer to be intimate was apparent. Even though I agreed, my thoughts were elsewhere. I felt misaligned and disconnected with the mood. It did not work! It just did not work!

As I ended the evening the revelation was as clear to me as the sun on a beautiful summer day, I was born for more than this. I could not believe that after I poured out my heart and shared intimate details of my life, secrets I never vocalized before my "friend" to such selfish acts, as if it were payment. I was done! I was completely done!

I spoke a truth to myself that night, like never in that moment. I was preaching. Undoubtedly, I was born for more than this. If I am good enough to take to dinner, I am good enough to marry. If I am good enough to go on a date, I am good enough to marry. If I am good enough to lay with, I am good enough to marry!

I continued this long enough to land on my knees with tears streaming from my eyes. My heart was pricked, and it changed instantaneously. My heart was bleeding the disgusting lies that I was not marriage material; that I was not good enough to marry; that I was not beautiful enough or thin enough to be a wife. I had to settle with used up garbage men.

I was coming out of a cocoon like a worm and transforming as a free flying beautiful butterfly. It was happening. What was? My past situations, set-ups and circumstances were changed! I was changed! What I once tolerated was evidently unacceptable and I was not taking it anymore.

That was the night, the day I vowed to celibacy and committed to God from the inside out. I was born for more than a side kick (side chick) or late-night swing. I was born to be great and much greater than where I was at that time. That day was my last day in that condition for surely, I was born for more. My expectations changed and now, I wanted more. I deserved more. I am worth MORE!

I Hated Me

I hated me.

It seems almost absurd to hate yourself as if you have offended or brought about turmoil to your own life. But there was a feeling inside of me that remained consistent and it was more forceful than discontentment and more agitating than dislike. That emotional response when I looked at myself in a mirror was hate.

I hated the curves of my hips because the style of clothing I desired never fit correctly. I hated the fullness of my breasts because the buttons on my shirt always opened unexpectantly. I hated the way my hair would fall because it was not long enough. I hated the way I talked and smiled automatically because it made me seem weak to strangers. I hated talking like a girl because the sound lacked authority. Every passive verb tense, every unassertive comment, and every submissive response annoyed me. I could hear the feminine sound in conversations and with disdain I learned how to speak directly, absent ambiguous innuendoes.

I hated it. I hated the way I would sound uncertain. I hated the way I lacked confidence when approached. It was because I was a girl and I hated that I was a girl and for that, I hated me, a girl!

I looked in the mirror and I did not like what was looking back at me. I could not stand looking at her face. Her facial features were despicable. I did not want her here anymore. I hated the beauty of my face and called it ugly! Ugly girl! I hated that ugly girl!

Anything that aligned with female inferiority I hated. I did not like flowers or pink. I shunned the pretty girl stuff and wanted to make my claim as a strong powerful woman. I hated my menstrual cycle and used birth control to put an end to it. I hated the idea of having a body with a reproductive system that prevented me from being free and safe. I had to check my environment when walking to my car at night. I had to hypervigilant when traveling alone as my gender, my sex, my being was inferior. I could not take it. I hated it. I hated me.

I experienced discrimination because I was a girl. I was denied access to sports and hobbies because I was a girl. I experienced lack and poverty because I was a girl. After I divorced my first husband, I became a single mother raising my son while attending college. I was poor, living off a student worker's wages. I did not like it. I hated it. I hated being a girl. I hated me.

That a woman could be excluded because she was a woman, but desired because she was a woman was contradictory. Engulfed by the racial slurs because of the color of my skin caused me to want out of my skin. The overwhelming biases toward women I faced daily resulted in my passionate desire to escape this thing called womanhood so I could have more, be more and be me. So, I hated it. I hated me, this me I was in.

Why was I not enough as a woman, as a girl? Why does the creation in my underwear dictate the extent of my power and well-being, my access and level of prosperity, my ability to overpower those made weaker than myself?

I hated what made me inferior and weak and I hated what made men strong and aggressive. It fed this sickness of hating myself and soon bled into a mutual disrespect for men.

All my hate toward men and all my hate towards being a girl was affixed to that moment in time when I was a girl, being molested, fondled, and touched unrighteous, unkindly, inappropriately. I believed that it happened because I was a girl. If I were a boy, it would not have happened. If I were not a girl, it would not have happened. While today I know this is a lie, much of my young adult life, it was my truth. It was that truth that made me free to hate, free to fight, and free to disregard the perfection of my make-up and my testimony. It was that truth that made my friends know I hated men and made men know they were unwelcomed in my space.

The intensity of the hate for self was debilitating. I could not grow like that. I could not praise like that. I could not live like that and I was raising a boy!

How would he survive the vicious unloving motives of a mother who could not see him as a positive influence on the world, but a piece of what was wrong in the world? How was he going to live through his mother's horror and tirades? With covered ears and a hardened heart. This woman, single mother raising a son, heartless, angry, and hopeless only God could save her. Only God could save them both!

50

The internal hatred changed. It became undying love. The path for this change included forgiving myself, primarily. Once I found the space and the compassion to acknowledge my pain and release it, I was prepared to forgive others and accept people as they were.

My journey out of self-hatred involved confrontation. I met in-person or by telephoned those I needed to ask for forgiveness. I called my former boyfriends and asked for forgiveness. I called my ex-husband and asked for forgiveness. I called my former lovers and asked for forgiveness. It was an exposing process to realize that my past behaviors, words, and thoughts were incorrect! I was humbled. I became pure and I no longer hated me or others!

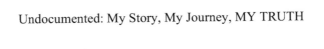

This time when the enemy swings, JUMP!

It's in the Ride

Sometimes it's in the ride! I didn't feel church tonight, way too much to do (write a paper, baby bath, homework, dinner, pay bills) and it's a 30-minute drive to church, but the Holy Spirit said, "Go!"

In the drive, I was given the gift of freedom and deliverance and healing. I received revelation from the Lord and words to hold me and keep me. It was in the ride that God visited me and released me from the strongholds I faced so my words to encourage you are

Sometimes, it's in the ride!

*I opened my eyes and there you were,
tomorrow.*

Who Are You?

Waking up and looking in the mirror left me confused. Who is that looking back at me? I did not recognize her. This was not the first time I saw her, but it was the first time I looked at her. She had been looking at me every day and every night for the past two years. She has been crying for attention and starving for love for the past two years. I would take a glance at the important parts. Her face was clean, her make-up planted lightly and inerrant, and her teeth were brushed. The rest were the daily hygiene formalities of lotion soap and water, let's go.

Where was she going every day? What was the hurry? What race was she running? Who was that girl?

It was a sad day the day she was seen by me. I saw her face and face paint, but it was her eyes, those eyes. I was not sure who that was in the mirror.

I did not recognize her smile. I did not recognize her look. I did not even recognize her face. I looked closer. I looked deeper. I took a picture. I looked at the picture and the picture looked back at me. I did not recognize her. I was not sure where she had come from or how she had arrived in my bathroom mirror. Is that me? Is that what I look like?

When did that happen? When did your face begin to frown like that? When did your skin complexion change? When did your body transform like that? When did this body form feel like this? Oh, who are you and how did you get here? Where have you been? Where did YOU come from?

I stared at her. I looked her over, up and down. Her cheeks looked different. Her smile made her face look weird. Her nose was placed awkwardly. Her skin tone was blemished and aging. Her eyes, I could not describe them. Her eyes were dark, almost black. Looking into them seemed empty yet mystical, it was like looking in a black hole. I could see nothing but the black emptiness that crept as her eyes looked back at me.

Her eyes were looking at me and I was looking at them in awe of how disconnected and misaligned she was. Her eyes made her look like she was heartless. That look of compassion and care was missing. It made me feel sorry for her. It made me feel scared for her. For a moment, I slightly startled myself as I gasped and thought, "Where was her soul?"

I was not there. I could hear the words of the preacher say, "Will the real DelShanna please stand up?" and immediately the epiphany was clear as sunshine. I was not me!

I lost her somewhere. I mean, I lost *me* somewhere. I do not know if it was the challenges of finding myself in the marriage and family culture or the dynamics of working in an occult environment. Daily I smiled. I entered the room and the appearance of joy came exuberantly through my presence. However, I was missing. Where was I? I could not discern if my smile were a defense mechanism covering the disgust I had for my life; or if it were that superficial professional smile used as a façade in the workplace.

I stood and looked at her for a few minutes. Hands on the countertop, intensely staring at who this woman was looking back at me and for the life of me. I could not figure out who she was.

Was I accepting the bondage of traditionalism and neglecting my purpose? Had I been hit by the pendulum of the 1950s and lost myself to the expectations of others? It was true, me was looking back at me, but I did not know who I was anymore. And I did not like what I saw. I did not like what I had seen. The depths of black eyes staring back at me looking at black eyes was waiting for the code to unlock the mystery and answer the question, "Who are you?"

Heal me, O Lord, and I will be healed; save me and I will be saved, for you are the one I praise." Jeremiah 17:14

That Anger Thing

I was furious. But I didn't know why
I was so angry I could cry.

Cry because I wanted to fight. I was ready to fight. I wanted to destroy something, break something, throw things about. I wanted to destroy someone, tear them apart.

If anyone said a word to me, they would get it! I was ready to release expletives of all sorts to express the level of rage roaring on the inside of me.

How could you?
Why would you?
How dare you?
Just who do you think you are?
You will never hurt me like that again?

And there it was. A return to my painful past. Back to the beginning, the root of which all my pain had dwelled. I was molested!

I am still angry! And sometimes I can contain it or talk myself out of the explosion, but when I can't, my Lord! These explosive moments are like a volcano erupting. Except I am a person, a human being, a woman. They incorporate all the negative perceptions, innuendos on conversations that were never clarified and of course all the unworthiness I still feel on the inside- as spoiled goods.

I spent years bottling it up. I ate to suppress it. I isolated myself to depress it. I even jumped into others trauma to reject it but when the smoke cleared and the trigger hit, EXPLOSION! I was still angry!

I was angry at everyone! I was angry at no one! I didn't even have a face to point my finger at when I yelled! I couldn't decipher/ differentiate between my friend or my foe. But what I knew was that I wasn't safe anymore and I couldn't cover that up and I could no longer hide that.

It's been a few decades since the abuse, but the unspoken secrets surrounding it remain. I am working through this anger so I can stop confusing my loved ones. They still don't understand what's wrong and I haven't figured out how to stop being so angry for things that only replace what caused me pain.

I'll tell you what, don't hit the trigger. I might not act like you think.

I am this woman, not that one.

I'm Okay

I am okay. I am satisfied with what I have. I am accepting of the life I live and those that live it with me. I am okay.

I am okay is usually one of the popular responses given when asked about your day. It is an unemotional, disconnected, politically accepted and dismissive response. On most days and in most cases, it is a bold face lie.

Truth is no one cares how you feel today. No one is going to lose sleep about your life or issues today. So, when asked about your feelings, the answer is simply, "I'm okay."

I heard my grandson say it one day. It was the cutest sound but left a disturbing ring in my ear. He was running, fell, got up and announced, "I'm okay. I'm okay Granny."

He had done it before. He had been trained to say so. It was expected that he down-play his injuries and mishaps. He had been taught that crying about pain was unacceptable. We have been taught to ignore or hide our pain because the natural response represents our inferior primal instinct. I was taught that discussing pain would not be tolerated and would never be publicly acknowledged.

The perpetuation of dishonesty seems to exist in the narrative to the receptor from acknowledging our humanity and our pain. It is this way so others may carry on with their day.

Have we become so faceless and heartless that we no longer genuinely display authentic relationship efforts such as listening, compassion, support, and care?

Well, I am okay. I am okay with the facts of who I am and who you are and are not. I am okay. I am okay with your lack and excess. I am okay with your strange fire and holy fire. I am okay.

I woke up one morning and decided that if you are happy with your lies and dysfunction, then so am I. I am okay. I am alright with the fake and the phony.

What I am not okay with is you pretending to love me or care about what happens to me or even support my projects. Wasn't I there for you? Wasn't I in the audience, cheering you on? Wasn't I the one that you called for suggestions and ideas? As a matter of fact, wasn't your multimillion-dollar program my idea in the first place? I am okay!

I am okay because I have my own groove. I am working my own life and I am walking my own journey. That is the power of being me, unapologetically and authentically.

I am okay with you just the way you are. No, no, please do not change. Do not change your hair, your look or even your attitude to impress me or sound better off than you are, stay you. Stay the way you were made up to be. Stay the way you have chosen to be. And while you are busy, and way too busy for me, I am okay. I am okay being me, just like me, unapologetically and authentically.

Life spared. Grace applied

I Feel

Tonight…
I feel.
I feel.
I feel for real.

I feel the pain, the hurt, the anxiety, and the embarrassment. I am sitting in front of the TV and crying. These tears are not the result of the awful events that have occurred to innocent beautiful children. These are not the tears of anger and revenge in hopes that justice is paid to the fullest. No! These are the tears of years of unaddressed sorrow and hidden woes. These are the tears of multiples losses in the company of people who would not let me cry. These are the tears of, the tears for and the tears because I am letting myself feel!

Oh, what pain to feel, for not being valued enough to be protected and kept safe. Oh, what fear to have for not knowing what they will do to me when they enter the room. Oh, what shame to embrace for not knowing how to feel clean enough after they touched me and made me dirty. Oh, how my heart breaks when they blame me for how they hurt me. I feel dirty, but it is not my fault. It was not my fault. I did nothing wrong, and I have no one to help me.

I gave myself permission to feel this, to feel all of it. Once I was given permission to feel, I realized it was and is okay to feel. It is okay to feel the horrifying stories of rapists abusing children. It was okay to feel the overwhelming fear of an abuser storming in the room to beat a child. It is okay to be overwhelmed with sorrow and grief trying to comprehend the psychological and emotional disconnection between humanity and the incomprehensible acts of perverted lasciviousness and physical abuse on children.

I can feel it now. I can feel it like it was me being spread open and torn apart, raised and beaten, rejected and destroyed by those who were placed in my life to nurture, protect, provide safety and loving care, the life guides, parents, adults, babysitters, coaches, foster caregiver, neighbors, relatives, and strangers.

It hurts to feel this immense pain. It hurts to know that the discomfort of my reality is only in thought while a little baby somewhere is experiencing this pain, defined as love, and named "my life." My eyes swelled up. And tears flow down my rounded cheeks as my heart cries out for help.

"HELP! HELP! Somebody, help me!!!"

"Can I get some protection here?"

"Will anyone stand up to protect me?
Is anyone there? Can you hear me cry?"

A listening ear. Will I have the right, the privilege to a listening ear? The type of ear that hears my pain and rescues me.

A security blanket. The type of security blanket that covers me up. That smooth comfort of a special blanket. That special blanket used to protect me from monsters in a cold and dark room, no one can see me, and the evil ones cannot touch me.

It hurts because it is real. It hurts because I feel it! No longer numb, I am alive.

Go where your favor carries you.

MY

TRUTH

Who Told You That?

Who told you, you were ugly? Tell them, I was created by power and designed in beauty. Ugly was never my name.

Who told you, you were fat? Tell them, I was created as an independent, unique, and irreplaceable blueprint in a world full of "wannabes". Fat was never my name.

Who told you, you were not worth it? Tell them, I was born into riches and raised in wealth. The wealth of my youth and the riches of my future are manifesting in my journey to greatness. Unworthy was never my name.

Who told you, you were undeserving? Tell them, I was created to have more than I could think or imagine. I was created to expect greatness, love, and respect. Undeserving was never my name.

Who told you, you were not enough? Tell them, I was born enough. God only made one of me, full and complete. There was never another nor will there ever be, another one of me.

Truth is, you are correct, I am not enough, I am more than enough. I am abundance. I am overflowing. I am effervescent. I am more than even you can think or imagine. My image is mystically undefinable by science and mankind. My existence and breath have yet to be reproduced or recreated.

In fact, tell them, "Try it! Try to make another me, a perfect me." They will discover that I am the discovery, the evidence, and the truth. Not enough was never my name.

In fact, all the names they called me were incorrect. I am she. I am her. I am DelShanna.

Unapologetically Authentically Me

Without apologizing for who I am, I am who I am. For some reason people have adopted a language that ensures they apologize for being who they are. Often, you'll hear someone say, "I'm sorry, but I...," when giving an opinion. Unfavorable opinions do not require an apology. In a culture that devalues different, it is imperative that we allow people to speak the truth. THEIR truth. Unapologetically.

Hope deferred makes the heart sick, but a longing fulfilled is a tree of life. Proverbs 13:12

The Girl I Love

There came a time when I had looked in the mirror and saw the softness and beauty of being a girl, a woman. When I did not like what I saw, I became angry with the lack of power of being a girl, feminine in stature, a woman. I could not be stronger than what I was. I could not be better than the woman I was made to be. I was frustrated with knowing there was greater, but I was unable to make it tangible, make it mine. However, what I did have changed my perspective.

Oftentimes we focus on the wrong thing and create a culture, philosophy, or lifestyle contrary to our purpose. I spent too much time wanting what I thought only a man could have. I spent too many emotions hating Myself. On this day, at this time, I woke up. I loved me!

I could see how the mysterious universal creator used majestic excellence to create me just as I was. Every curve and giggle were purposely positioned to make me. Every life experience, traumatic scene I could recall was purposed just for me to have and to hold. I looked at people differently. I saw how God made everyone and everything and "it was very good" (Genesis 1:31).

Yes, every single person on earth from yesterday, today, and tomorrow was designed with perfection in mind. The ugliness I once focused on was no longer a thought in my mind. I would smile at strangers and think, "how wonderful are the works of the Lord" (Psalm 92:5). Even that scar on a face, amputee and awkward shaped body was purposed by design. Wow! What a relief to consider the positive perspective of life, of my life and of my life experience.

It was easy making this transition in my thoughts because I am genuinely a positive fun-loving type of gal. The hard part was reminding myself thousands of times every day that there was a positive side to what was being presented. There was a good thing in who was before me. There was divine purpose in what was happening. I was finally accepting and loving the girl that I was.

Sometimes I fall back into the hateful thinking, but through His word I have found thoughts to consider and things to think about that are more aligned with HIS will than my ego or emotional inconsistencies. Part of the Daily Journey Devotion found in Philippians 4, gives a list of things to think about (Moore, 2016). Trouble, war time and unrestful moments are expected. However, this passage of scripture is a prescription, the medicine to live better. How? Simply read and recite the scripture:

> *And now, dear brothers and sisters, one final thing. Fix your thoughts on what is true, and honorable, and right, and pure, and lovely, and admirable. Think about things that are excellent and worthy of praise (Philippians 4:8, NLT).*

The scripture does not then spell out what not to think about, but trust to know that assumed opposites of the expected thoughts is a spiritual problem. Think about it? Why would you think about things that were false, lies, impure, dirty, unrighteous, hateful, a bad report or story that is absent praise and virtue. That would cause us trauma and stress, much like the evening news does, right?

It took scripture to fight away impure thoughts about being a girl. Even though I was mishandled and touched perversely as a child, it did not make me an inferior creature or spoiled goods. Instead, it made me strong, wise, and powerful beyond measure. I continue to strive to live out the powerful access I have, but in the meantime, I press on with joy to be who I am, who I was created to be and to be a girl, the girl that I love.

I Forgive Me

I forgive you for hurting me.
I forgive you for not hearing me.
I forgive you for not knowing.
I forgive you for not knowing better.
I forgive you for following the leader.
I forgive you for doing what was done to you.
I forgive you for practicing on me.
I forgive you for disrespecting me.
I forgive you for not believing me.
I forgive you for not being trustworthy.
I forgive you for not protecting me.
I forgive you for touching me.
I forgive you for using me.
I forgive you for showing me that.
I forgive you for what they did to me.
I forgive you for participating.
I forgive you for not telling.
I forgive you for that bad advice.
I forgive you for doing nothing.
I forgive you for leaving me.
I forgive you for everything.
I forgive me.

The pursuit of happiness is freedom.
Freedom encourages joy.
Joy overflows and infects everything.

Freedom

What does freedom feel like? For real. How does it feel to feel free? How does it feel to be free?

I never knew I was bound. I did not know I had chains blocking me from going forward, stopping me from moving at all. But they were there. At first, they were invisible. I could not see what was preventing me from growing and moving and forming into a well-developed emotionally mature young woman. I did not understand why I could see the glimpse of happiness, but not have it. It did not make sense why I could help others reach their destination and sit back and never get anywhere near my own.

Was it my size? Was I too fat to be the one chosen or too voluptuous to be the one in front? Did my size matter so much that I lost access to what was undeniably mine?

Was it my skin color? With the antics of racism, colorism, and nationalism, maybe it was the tone of my skin or the shine of my hair or the tightened curls on the back of my neck that made them deny me access to my throne.

Was it my move? The way I entered a room or the way I shifted to make my exit. Was I too quiet or too loud? Was my language improper or ghetto or too colorful? Were the words used incomprehensible or was I speaking in code?

What was it about me, DelShanna, that wouldn't let me have what I wanted, what I dreamed about, what I could see and reach for, but could not obtain? What was it?

It was those chains that bound me to the scared little girl who was not beloved and had no voice. Those near me could hear my shout of instruction motivating them cheering them on from the stands, pushing them to press through the crowd for their success. But what about me?

Were their eardrums attuned to my cry for help, my cry for deliverance or my cry for support to gain access to my dreams and my future greatness. Those chains were heavy. They were thick. They were bigger than I. They were stronger than I.

I desired to pull them off, but I could not see them. Where were they? I knew something heavy was holding me down. I knew something stronger was holding me back. Then I experienced blurred vision, the appearance of the strongholds that had me bound. My eyes were keen enough, mature enough, and old enough showing me I could see how they interlocked throughout themselves making a bond I could not break alone.

What is freedom if I am locked up? What is freedom if I am locked out? What is freedom if I am locked in?

I needed help! I had a dream about a man who removed dead bodies off me. I could feel the weight of the bodies being lifted in the dream as if I were wide awake. One by one this man pulled dead bodies off me.

Years later I met this man. He was a Pastor. And just like my dream he pastored me, and piece by piece pulled off dead things in my life. He was a promise fulfilled, a dream come true, because in fact, the dream did come true.

But it was not all him. Even with dead weight removed there was a barrier I had to

Undocumented: My Story, My Journey, MY TRUTH

expose, a barrier that would not let me leap! It was invisible! It was big! It was strong! It was permanent?

I could not bounce back nor bounce into this free thing others experienced. Yes, the dead weight was gone, but this new-found freedom I had dreamed about was not any closer than before. That was when I realized I was chained up and free. What! How can you be free and bound? Easy. The pressure of the dead weight had been lifted, but the mental confinement remained.

What does freedom feel like? I did not know. I did not know because my feelings were not free. I had to address my weights emotionally, financially, relationally, and physically. Every facet of my life required keys to unlock the chains that held me back. The key is that I wanted it. I wanted to be free. At least I thought I did, until freedom began to present itself in my life like a best friend. Then, I realized, even with freedom within reach and chasing me, I began running from it because it was unfamiliar. I never had freedom before. I had been married to bondage and chains for so long that when freedom showed up, I ran.

What does freedom feel like? Like for real. How does it feel to feel free? How does it feel to be free?

Freedom is that best friend who holds every secret sacred and every conversation confidential. You can tell it all – that's freedom!

Freedom is the unfamiliarity of a wrapped gift. Something new unexpectantly expected awaiting its presentation before others like the birth of a newborn child – that's freedom!

Freedom is breath, air moving fluidly between substance and around barriers; never stopping, ignoring every red light, not hindered by mountains, or negative circumstances, yet moving upward.

Freedom is me.

Today, I am loved! I am enough! I am worth it!
For every blessing of health and well-being,
Lord, I thank you!

That Oil

I want to be dipped in the type of oil that changes my taste buds, changes what satisfies me and changes my life!

There is a substance that when used represents that supernatural connection between a prayer and the answer. It is found in the oil. The blessed oil that lies at the pulpit in the sanctuary or the prayer room of an intercessor. It is oil that when touched, heaven and earth collide and miracles, signs and wonders manifest in our life.

Biblically, the oil was a special blend used to anoint the tabernacle and sanctify Kingdom leaders (Ex. 30:22-33, Lev. 8:10-12, 1 Sam. 10:1, 1 Kings 1:39, Heb. 1:8-9). The oil identified the holy ones and reflected the covenant-keeping God.

It may look like mere olive oil in a jar, but its capacity to accent food, stimulate the palate, and enhance the smell and taste of food is incomparable. A class of its own, the oil leaves a residue of illuminating glory. It is self-rejuvenating and maintains strength to rebuild.

No matter the pressure accompanied by pulling, picking, shaking, tossing, and boiling temperatures, it fulfills its expectations. It changes things. It is that oil, anointed oil.

> *I want to be engulfed in the type of oil that changes what I thirst and hunger after, changes what I reach for, and changes what I chase after.*

The oil was me. While oil is not the substance I am made from, symbolically it represents who I am. I am oil. I am the substance who serves as a point of contact to the Lord. I am the very pressed and processed material needed to shift atmospheres and move mountains in my life and yours. I am the very strength needed to carry, pull up and push out. I am the oil. I am the little something that will cover you and encourage you to have the tenacity to continue to pursue the will of the Lord! I am the oil; the thing God uses to remind you of Him!

> *I want to be the type of oil that reroutes your journey and leads you to worship!*

I am the oil.

I am Living

It was a new environment, a place I had never been before. As I felt welcomed, I began to respond to the environment. I said, "Oh I am sorry." Someone heard me. They said, "You don't have to apologize for being you." "In fact," she said, "stop apologizing." I got it almost instantaneously. I knew exactly what she was talking about. She was acknowledging that somewhere in my DNA, my makeup was disallowing me to accept me for who I am, who I was. Instead I would ask permission to have an opinion, to share my truth, to be me. I got it! And that was the last time I said, "Oh, I'm sorry," after I made a comment or sharing my perspective.

Why? Because I was not sorry for how I felt. I was not apologizing for how I perceive the situation. I was not inferior in thought or purpose. I was as strong as and as smart as everyone else and so I began to be unapologetically authentically me!

Clearly, an apology may be warranted when offensive blatant vulgar obscenities are being used. However, is not necessarily desired or expected when describing who you are or what you believe or think to be true. Apologizing is the act of requesting forgiveness for wrongdoing or inability to perform. Why would we need to apologize for being who we are? Why would I need to apologize for being me?

So, I stopped! I stopped apologizing. I stood flat feet to the ground, shoulders squared and accepted my ME-ness. I accepted me for who I am, TODAY! Sure, I have goals for personal improvement, but until they manifest, I am here.

So, I will not apologize for the width of my nose, the length of my mouth, the size of my eyes or the shape of my body, the slang in my speech or the colloquialisms I use or the wrong words I say or the color or shade of my skin, where my parents came from or the city I live. I am unapologetically authentically ME!

I will not apologize for the political party I declare, the texture of my hair, my vote for President, or my favorite fragrance; my views on race, sex and gender or our disagreement with my convictions, for loving the way I do or separating from the wrong crowd, for not drinking alcohol, being short instead of tall; for being too smart or too dumb, for having a daughter and a son, for having the favor of God and man or receiving a pass by the police man.

Nope, I am not going to do it no more. No more apology from me! I am living my life authentically, unapologetically authentically ME!

LORD be gracious to us; we long for you. Be our strength every morning, our salvation in time of distress. Isaiah 33:2

I Trust Not

I do not know yawl. I walked away from a leadership class thinking after all this time, I still do not trust NOBODY! Processing it with my husband, I was honest to say that even if trust is earned in one moment, it is nontransferable, and people must re-earn my trust in every experience. Why? Because I was molested and the leaders in my life failed to protect me!

Even though I have counseled others, hand-held victims through healing and even deliverance. I am revered as trustworthy, but I trust not.

When my trust was broken as a child, I could not discern who to trust. I no longer carried the strong innocence of a child's senses that cried in the presence of a stranger or ran for Mommy when someone or something scary came around. I no longer had the ability to know if the people around me were loving or preying. I lived in fear, immense fear.

Trouble to me, meant that I could be abused again. Disappointment set me up for an act of abuse. Not meeting expectations meant abuse was imminent. I would be hurt for this. I earned it. It was going to be my fault, this time.

No one did it. Time and again I was free of the abuser and nothing bad happened to me. But I thought I was hurt because I was a bad girl. It kept happening because I was a bad girl. I could not talk about it because I was a bad girl.

My recollection of the thoughts and conclusions as a child are almost always incorrect. However, without the intellect of trusted elders, who could have convinced me that what I thought was all wrong?

I grew up absent of the ability to know how to trust my instincts. They were knocked into confusion by the abuser. I lost that piece of the normal developmental process from childhood to adulthood. I had to learn it as an adult.

I had the help of a therapist and some fabulous college friends. Strangers at first, we became a family of misfits who genuinely loved each other and all our flaws, inadequacies, and deficiencies. In this family, I could trust. I learned trust and practiced trusting my instincts and no one was hurt. No one was hurt again.

However, I also learned that as I entered new relationships, trust was an uphill mountain of work to reach and maintain. I even came face-to-face with the lack of trust I had with God. I would receive a word through prayer about something good was going to happen in my life and I would immediately disregard. It was as if it was not for me, really. I did not believe it.

My consistent thoughts were, "Yea, you're saying that, but you are not really going to do it, for me."

Was God a liar? Never. But the relationship I had with distrust was so consuming that I had no idea I was positioned in a trusted place, with trustworthy people and in the presence of a never-failing God.

Because lack of trust has been my greatest defense in a harsh, brutal, and unforgiving world, it has also been my greatest barrier to being vulnerably awesome, just the way God made me! There is a little genius inside of me screaming to get out! Let Me Go! SET ME FREE! *FATHER HELP!*

I Am Who I Am

Today I killed it! I entered the room and it lit up looking back at me. Because I killed it! I entertained conversations about change, help, assistance, and progress. I killed it! My attitude was gracious, yet stern. My expectations were clear and convincing. My love was evident and pure.

Was it the sound of my move, shifting from left to, right? Or was it the wind that clearly assisted my embrace for a new look on this new day? Was it the look or truly the internal confidence that comes with knowing exactly what to do? Or was it knowing exactly how to do it and doing it in such a way that even your enemies congratulate you and speak of your good, thereby overshadowing your bad?

Like with most demonstrations of confidence and self-love, you awaken the truth of who you are, and you walk like who you are. It was easy to walk behind others and hide in their overbearing shadows. It is difficult to be me. Being me is accepting my perks and flaws. Being me is being satisfied with the unacceptable and incomprehensible as well as exploring and exposing the greatest parts of my personality, size, look and attitude.

Here is the truth. Here is to my truth, I am who I am, period.

That's Me

I am my size and that's me. If I don't like it, I'll change it. If I don't like it, but I accept it, then that's me. That's who I am.

I am my color and that's me. If I don't like it, I'll change it. If I don't like it, but I accept It, then that's me. That's who I am.

I am my kinky coiled hair. If I don't like it, I'll change it. If I don't like it, but I accept it, then that's me. That's who I am.

I am my effervescent personality and that's me. If I don't like it, I believe I'll change it. If I don't like it, but I accept it, then that's me. That's who I am.

I am my rigid perspective and book-based decision-making self. If I don't like it, I'll change it. If I don't like it, but I accept it, then that's me. That's who I am.

I am my loving, caring and protective self. If I don't like it, I'll change it. If I don't like it, but I accept it, then that's me. That's who I am.

I am who I am. If I don't like it, I'll change it. If I don't like it, but I accept it, then that's me. That's who I am.

I am just that, me, unapologetically, authentically me.

That's Me!

Protector

It was clear after the session that I had a core value guiding me. This core value was the measure used to influence my decisions, relationships, career choice, volunteer work, ministry, and everything I was involved in. I held leadership positions in program areas that centered around this core value. The volunteer groups, employment, and entrepreneur ventures, as well as ministry was all connected. Once I could name this core value, the epiphany struck like lightening, awakening an understanding in my life I never knew. The essence of who I am and all in which I participated shared a thread thickened by this core value. The value uncovered in my core was that I am a protector.

I had it wrong for many years. I was mistaken. I would recite my passion to help people as my ultimate purpose and destiny in life. I would agree to multiple projects at one time because I wanted to help people. I found myself neglecting my work, ministry, and family because I believed I was called to help people. I was helping people recover from setbacks, establish systematic business practices, rekindle their marriages, and embrace love again. It was good work! It was helpful and people's lives were changing. I loved it! I was "helping people!"

But why? Why was I especially committed to their cause and projects and neglecting my own? Why was I searching for resolution for them and not even addressing my own deficiencies? What was causing me to immediately respond to their cry for help? That what, that why, was the protector in me.

I was running to their rescue. I was protecting them from the monsters that stir when someone does not respond to the cry for help! I was helping them stay safe, stay protected.

I wanted them to be free of the pain of discipline and hurt. I wanted them to not have to experience the suffering and loneliness I once felt. I wanted to make sure they were out of harm's way and covered if harm came their way. I wanted to protect them.

Funny thing, I was not very adamant about protecting me. You would think after many years of pain, hurt and disappointment and attempts of others to destroy me that I would take every precaution to protect myself, but no, I would stand in the way as a sacrifice to make sure others were protected.

I noticed how others did not do that. I realized how no one was doing that for me. Incident after incident, I walked away beaten and torn while others remained untouched. I made it look like glee and happiness. I made it look like learning and progress, but I was wounded. I was bleeding. I was hurt. And because my core was to protect, I had no choice but to continue to protect. I had to be the one to stand in the way and the gap to make sure others had what they needed. They had to be satisfied and okay. But what about me? What about me!

Silence (Selah)

I put myself out there. No one asked me to, they never had to ask. At the mention of the problems, I found myself calculating how I could protect. Even when the people I was protecting were hurting me and speaking of me negatively, tearing a hole in my reputation and my heart, I continued to develop strategies to safeguard them and not myself.

The day it caught up with me I pulled off the sheets, blankets and covers. I was angry and sad and told it all. That selfless devotion that used to wrap me in guilt and shame had been cut off. No longer was I required to pour out my pearls or give away all my oil, so they did not go without. I had my pearls and oil for myself!

I had access to share, but not give away completely. I had rights and privileges to protect and share, but not deplete. That core value was not for them only. Being a protector was for me, too.

You do not get a reward for protecting people, you get a battle scar.

I stopped protecting them and I started protecting me. How? Boundaries, boundaries, boundaries! This change was not met with a celebratory event, sympathy cards for my loss nor encouraging words to accompany my new-found revelation to take care of me. No one gave me a pat on the back. No one offered a big genuine hug. No one even noticed I had changed, except me. And that was enough.

<u>C*A*L*L T*O A*C*T*I*O*N</u>

Say Something! Do Something! Let's go!

For decades and now into the new century, children and women remain the degraded, discounted, ignored, and preyed upon. From the molestation and rape of children, impregnation of teens and sex trafficking that exists all over the world, it is disheartening that the smartest species on the globe can perpetuate such inhumane behavior. The treatment of sex slaves like animals and children being sold for family sustenance, enough is enough.

While we may not be able to resolve every issue incorporated with sexual abuse of the vulnerable, we can better publicize the pure disregard and destruction of basic human rights. Yes! TELL!!!!

This is your job! This is your neighbors' job! You have a responsibility to report threats of harm to the vulnerable and create safe communities for those who have been victimized, raped, abused, and trafficked.
While so many try to reconstruct the virtue of innocent children, others work to heal

the scars of continuous abuse in hopes to restore "life and the pursuit of happiness." However, exposing the villains, requires sleepless nights and persistent support until justice is served, protection is given, and peace is restored to the families traumatized by such inhuman activities.

Will you help save the next baby from a mother's angry boyfriend? Will you help rescue an eight (8) year old girl from being raped repeatedly by a family member or neighbor? Will you help save those beautiful teenage girls and boys from being preyed upon by a socially accepted pedophile? Will you help redeem young men and women from the snare of sex traffickers, pimps, johns, kidnappers, and murderers?

You have the power to change this world one child, youth, and victim at a time. You can see something and be the one who makes the call that saves a generation of disenfranchised people who require rehabilitation, recovery, and support. I believe it is possible! I know it is possible! You the fight to rescue our loved ones and the loved ones of others by learning more and making the call!

Go to:

National Sexual Assault
1-800-656-HOPE (4673)

National Human (Sex) Trafficking
1-888-373-7888

National Homeless Youth Hotline
1-800-RUNAWAY

National Child Abuse Hotline
1-800-4-A-CHILD (800-422-4453)

National Domestic Violence Hotline
1-800-799-7233

American Civil Liberties Union (ACLU)
1-212-549-2500

<u>Make the movement eradicate the destruction of our babies today!</u>

Commit!

COMMITMENT

If you are or know someone who has been abused, raped, preyed upon, beaten or forced into prostitution or sex trafficking, share the aforementioned information in a safe space and accompany them to support groups, advocates, and agencies.

Make your commitment to help by completing the following:

I, _____, make a commitment effective this _____ day of _____ 20__, to call officials when I see or hear of a child, youth or young person being abused, and when possible, I will make financial and volunteer contributions to legitimate agencies in the fight against abuse and trafficking.

_____   _____
Signature   **Date**

References

"BibleHub Passage" www.biblehub.com, N.p. 2020.

Holy Bible, New Living Translation, (2015). Tyndale House Foundation. Tyndale House Publishers, Inc., Carol Stream, Illinois

Journey from Salvation to Worship (2016). Moore, DelShanna. Get Write Publishing. Dallas, TX.

www.1800runaway.org, (2020). National Homeless Youth Hotline.

www.aclu.org, (2020). American Civil Liberties Union (ACLU).

www.childhelp.org, (2020). National Child abuse Hotline.

www.humantraffickinghotline.com, (2020). National Human (Sex) Trafficking.

www.rainn.org, (2020). National Sexual Assault Hotline.

www.thehotline.org, (2020). National Domestic Violence Hotline.

Take the Journey from Salvation to Worship

The *Journey from Salvation to Worship is a daily devotional guide accompanied by a thought-provoking workbook.* These books guide you through scriptures used as your daily prescription for freedom, wholeness and intimacy with God. Repetitiously reading scripture as and answering workbook questions foster a relationship with God that will facilitate spiritual growth for Believers of all levels of maturity. A testament to learning about the Bible, understanding scripture and addressing your weaknesses, issues and struggles, the Journey from Salvation to Worship depicts DelShanna Moore's return with a deliberate provoking process to move Christians to a deeper level of intimacy with Christ.

Order copies today at
https://www.iamwrappedinhisword.com

DelShanna Moore

DelShanna Moore experienced self-destructive behaviors and enticement with perversion and alcohol. She facilitates workshops as a pathway to reconciliation, deliverance, and restoration. She exposes God's Word in a way that pierces the stony heart, shatters the walls of alienation, and connects you to the freedom granted by the Spirit. She is a certified Life Coach, ordained minister and achieved dual degrees in Psychology and Public Administration from the University of Nevada Las Vegas.

Reading her books, attending her training courses, or listening to her speak, leaves you with the phenomenal impression of God's undeniable love and compassion. Receiving divine intervention and 'loosing' captives proves she is a phenomenal transformational catalyst ready to change your world.

Connect with DelShanna Moore
(702) 525-0139
https://www.iamwrappedinhisword.com

I acknowledge my value.
I embrace my beauty.
I accept my favor.
I am unapologetically authentically ME

Made in the USA
Coppell, TX
08 October 2020